NEW SELECTED POEMS

John Montague

NEW
SELECTED
POEMS

BLOODAXE BOOKS
GALLERY BOOKS

Copyright © John Montague 1961, 1967, 1970, 1972,
1975, 1977, 1978, 1984, 1988, 1989, 1990

ISBN 1 85224 113 6 hardback edition
      1 85224 114 4 paperback edition

This edition published 1990 by
Bloodaxe Books Ltd,
P.O. Box 1SN,
Newcastle upon Tyne NE99 1SN,
in England, Wales & Scotland
in association with The Gallery Press.

Bloodaxe Books Ltd acknowledges
the financial assistance of Northern Arts.

This book was first published
in 1989 by The Gallery Press,
edited and designed by Peter Fallon,
and originated in Ireland.
The publishers acknowledge
the contribution of Dillon Johnston
towards the selection of these poems.

Printed in Great Britain by
Billing & Sons Ltd, Worcester

Contents

for Seamus Montague

The Water Carrier

Twice daily I carried water from the spring,
Morning before leaving for school, and evening;
Balanced as a fulcrum between two buckets.

A bramble rough path ran to the river
Where you stepped carefully across slime-topped stones,
With corners abraded as bleakly white as bones.

At the widening pool (for washing and cattle)
Minute fish flickered as you dipped,
Circling to fill, with rust-tinged water.

The second or enamel bucket was for spring water
Which, after racing through a rushy meadow,
Came bubbling in a broken drain-pipe,

Corroded wafer thin with rust.
It ran so pure and cold, it fell
Like manacles of ice on the wrists.

You stood until the bucket brimmed
Inhaling the musty smell of unpicked berries,
That heavy greenness fostered by water.

Recovering the scene, I had hoped to stylize it,
Like the portrait of an Egyptian water-carrier:
But pause, entranced by slight and memoried life.

I sometimes come to take the water there,
Not as return or refuge, but some pure thing,
Some living source, half-imagined and half-real,

Pulses in the fictive water that I feel.

Like Dolmens Round my Childhood, the Old People

Like dolmens round my childhood, the old people.

Jamie MacCrystal sang to himself,
A broken song without tune, without words;
He tipped me a penny every pension day,
Fed kindly crusts to winter birds.
When he died, his cottage was robbed,
Mattress and money-box torn and searched.
Only the corpse they didn't disturb.

Maggie Owens was surrounded by animals,
A mongrel bitch and shivering pups,
Even in her bedroom a she-goat cried.
She was a well of gossip defiled,
Fanged chronicler of a whole countryside;
Reputed a witch, all I could find
Was her lonely need to deride.

The Nialls lived along a mountain lane
Where heather bells bloomed, clumps of foxglove.
All were blind, with Blind Pension and Wireless,
Dead eyes serpent-flicked as one entered
To shelter from a downpour of mountain rain.
Crickets chirped under the rocking hearthstone
Until the muddy sun shone out again.

Mary Moore lived in a crumbling gatehouse,
Famous as Pisa for its leaning gable.
Bag-apron and boots, she tramped the fields
Driving lean cattle from a miry stable.
A by-word for fierceness, she fell asleep
Over love stories, *Red Star* and *Red Circle*,
Dreamed of gypsy love rites, by firelight sealed.

Wild Billy Eagleson married a Catholic servant girl
When all his Loyal family passed on:
We danced round him shouting 'To Hell with King Billy',
And dodged from the arc of his flailing blackthorn.
Forsaken by both creeds, he showed little concern
Until the Orange drums banged past in the summer
And bowler and sash aggressively shone.

Curate and doctor trudged to attend them,
Through knee-deep snow, through summer heat,
From main road to lane to broken path,
Gulping the mountain air with painful breath.
Sometimes they were found by neighbours,
Silent keepers of a smokeless hearth,
Suddenly cast in the mould of death.

Ancient Ireland, indeed! I was reared by her bedside,
The rune and the chant, evil eye and averted head,
Fomorian fierceness of family and local feud.
Gaunt figures of fear and of friendliness,
For years they trespassed on my dreams,
Until once, in a standing circle of stones,
I felt their shadows pass

Into that dark permanence of ancient forms.

Woodtown Manor

for Morris Graves

1
Here the delicate dance of silence,
The quick step of the robin,
The sudden skittering rush of the wren:
Minute essences move in and out of creation
Until the skin of soundlessness forms again.

Part order, part wilderness,
Water creates its cadenced illusion
Of glaucous, fluent growth;
Fins raised, as in a waking dream,
Bright fish probe their painted stream.

Imaginary animals harbour here:
The young fox coiled in its covert,
Bright-eyed and mean, the baby bird:
The heron, like a tilted italic,
Illuminating the gospel of the absurd.

And all the menagerie of the living marvellous:
Stone shape of toad,
Flicker of insect life,
Shift of wind touched grass
As though a beneficient spirit stirred.

2
Twin deities hover in Irish air
Reconciling poles of east and west;
The detached and sensual Indian God,
Franciscan dream of gentleness:
Gravity of Georgian manor
Approves, with classic stare,
Their dual disciplines of tenderness.

The Trout

Flat on the bank I parted
Rushes to ease my hands
In the water without a ripple
And tilt them slowly downstream
To where he lay, tendril light
In his fluid sensual dream.

Bodiless lord of creation
I hung briefly above him
Savouring my own absence
Senses expanding in the slow
Motion, the photographic calm
That grows before action.

As the curve of my hands
Swung under his body
He surged, with visible pleasure.
I was so preternaturally close
I could count every stipple
But still cast no shadow, until

The two palms crossed in a cage
Under the lightly pulsing gills.
Then (entering my own enlarged
Shape, which rode on the water)
I gripped. To this day I can
Taste his terror on my hands.

All Legendary Obstacles

All legendary obstacles lay between
Us, the long imaginary plain,
The monstrous ruck of mountains
And, swinging across the night,
Flooding the Sacramento, San Joaquin,
The hissing drift of winter rain.

All day I waited, shifting
Nervously from station to bar
As I saw another train sail
By, the *San Francisco Chief* or
Golden Gate, water dripping
From great flanged wheels.

At midnight you came, pale
Above the negro porter's lamp.
I was too blind with rain
And doubt to speak, but
Reached from the platform
Until our chilled hands met.

You had been travelling for days
With an old lady, who marked
A neat circle on the glass
With her glove, to watch us
Move into the wet darkness
Kissing, still unable to speak.

That Room

Side by side on the narrow bed
We lay, like chained giants,
Tasting each other's tears, in terror
Of the news which left little to hide
But our two faces that stared
To ritual masks, absurd and flayed.

Rarely in a lifetime comes such news
Shafting knowledge straight to the heart
Making shameless sorrow start —
Not childish tears, querulously vain —
But adult tears that hurt and harm,
Seeping like acid to the bone.

Sound of hooves on the midnight road
Raised a romantic image to mind:
The Dean riding late to Marley?
But we must suffer the facts of self.
No one endures a similar fate
And no one will ever know

What happened in that room
But when we came to leave
We scrubbed each other's tears,
Prepared the usual show. That day
Love's claims made chains of time and place
To bind us together more: equal in adversity.

The Water's Edge

Two of your landscapes I take —
The long loneliness of *Berck-Plage*
Where you walked, in your plaid uniform,
Directly into the wind.

Or the formal procession
Of horses, under the pale oaks
Of that urban forest where
You first learnt to ride.

There is in love that brief
Jealousy of the other's past
Coming on the charred roots
Of feeling, of ancient grief;

And here, in a third place,
Two of your landscapes seem to join
In a sweet conspiracy of mirrored
Surfaces, to baffle time

As the now heraldic animal
Stands by the water's edge
Lifting its rider against the sky,
A sudden shield.

The Country Fiddler

My uncle played the fiddle — more elegantly the violin —
A favourite at barn and crossroads dance,
He knew *The Sailor's Bonnet* and *The Fowling Piece*.

Bachelor head of a house full of sisters,
Runner of poor racehorses, spendthrift,
He left for the New World in an old disgrace.

He left his fiddle in the rafters
When he sailed, never played afterwards;
A rural art silenced in the discord of Brooklyn.

A heavily-built man, tranquil-eyed as an ox,
He ran a wild speakeasy, and died of it.
During the Depression many dossed in his cellar.

I attended his funeral in the Church of the Redemption,
Then, unexpected successor, reversed time
To return where he had been born.

During my schooldays the fiddle rusted
(The bridge fell away, the catgut snapped)
Reduced to a plaything stinking of stale rosin.

The country people asked if I also had music
(All the family had had) but the fiddle was in pieces
And the rafters remade, before I discovered my craft.

Twenty years afterwards, I saw the church again,
And promised to remember my burly godfather
And his rural craft, after this fashion:

So succession passes, through strangest hands.

Hill Field

All that bone bright winter's day
He completed my angle of sight
Patterning the hill field
With snaky furrows,
The tractor chimney smoking
Like his pipe, under the felt hat.

Ten years ago, it was a team
With bulky harness and suckling step
That changed our hill:
Grasping the cold metal
The tremble of the earth
Seemed to flow into one's hands.

Still the dark birds shape
Away as he approaches
To sink with a hovering
Fury of open beaks —
Starling, magpie, crow ride
A gunmetal sheen of gaping earth.

The Road's End

May, and the air is light
On eye, on hand. As I take
The mountain road, my former step
Doubles mine, driving cattle
To the upland fields. Between
Shelving ditches of whitethorn
They sway their burdensome
Bodies, tempted at each turn
By hollows of sweet grass,
Pale clover, while memory,
A restive sally-switch, flicks
Across their backs.
                         The well
Is still there, a half-way mark
Between two cottages, opposite
The gate into Danaghy's field,
But above the protective dry-
Stone rim, the plaiting thorns
Have not been bill-hooked back
And a thick glaur floats.
No need to rush to head off
The cattle from sinking soft
Muzzles into leaf-smelling
Spring water.
                         From the farm
Nearby, I hear a yard tap gush
And a collie bark, to check
My presence. Our farmhands
Lived there, wife and children
In twin white-washed cells,
A zinc roof burning in summer.
Now there is a kitchen extension
With radio aerial, rough outhouses

For coal and tractor. A housewife
Smiles good-day as I step through
The fluff and dust of her walled
Farmyard, solicited by raw-necked
Stalking turkeys;
                                to where cart
Ruts shape the ridge of a valley,
One of many among the switch-
Back hills of what old chroniclers
Called the Star Bog. Croziered
Fern, white scut of *ceannbhán*,
Spars of bleached bog fir jutting
From heather, make a landscape
So light in wash it must be learnt
Day by day, in shifting detail.
'I like to look across,' said
Barney Horisk, leaning on his *sleán*,
'And think of all the people
Who have bin.'
                                Like shards
Of a lost culture, the slopes
Are strewn with cabins, emptied
In my lifetime. Here the older
People sheltered, the Blind Nialls,
Big Ellen, who had been a Fair-
Day prostitute. The bushes cramp
To the evening wind as I reach
The road's end. Jamie MacCrystal
Lived in the final cottage,
A trim grove of mountain ash
Soughing protection round his walls
And bright painted gate. The thatch
Has slumped in, white dust of nettles

On the flags. Only the shed remains
In use for calves, although fuchsia
Bleeds by the wall, and someone
Has propped a yellow cartwheel
Against the door.

A Bright Day

for John McGahern

At times I see it, present
   As a bright day, or a hill,
The only way of saying something
   Luminously as possible.

Not the accumulated richness
   Of an old historical language —
That musk-deep odour!
   But a slow exactness

Which recreates experience
   By ritualizing its details —
Pale web of curtain, width
   Of deal table, till all

Takes on a witch-bright glow
   And even the clock on the mantel
Moves its hands in a fierce delight
   Of so, and so, and so.

A Chosen Light

1   II RUE DAGUERRE
At night, sometimes, when I cannot sleep
I go to the *atelier* door
And smell the earth of the garden.

It exhales softly,
Especially now, approaching springtime,
When tendrils of green are plaited

Across the humus, desperately frail
In their passage against
The dark, unredeemed parcels of earth.

There is white light on the cobblestones
And in the apartment house opposite —
All four floors — silence.

In that stillness — soft but luminously exact,
A chosen light — I notice that
The tips of the lately grafted cherry-tree

Are a firm and lacquered black.

2   SALUTE, IN PASSING

for Samuel Beckett

The voyagers we cannot follow
Are the most haunting. That face
Time has worn to a fastidious mask
Chides me, as one strict master
Steps through the Luxembourg.
Surrounded by children, lovers,
His thoughts are rigorous as trees
Reduced by winter. While the water

Parts for tiny white-rigged yachts
He plots an icy human mathematics —
Proving what content sighs when all
Is lost, what wit flares from nothingness:
His handsome Aztec head is sacrificial
As he weathers to how man now is.

The Cage

My father, the least happy
man I have known. His face
retained the pallor
of those who work underground:
the lost years in Brooklyn
listening to a subway
shudder the earth.

But a traditional Irishman
who (released from his grille
in the Clark St. I.R.T.)
drank neat whiskey until
he reached the only element
he felt at home in
any longer: brute oblivion.

And yet picked himself
up, most mornings,
to march down the street
extending his smile
to all sides of the good,
all-white neighbourhood
belled by St. Teresa's church.

When he came back
we walked together
across fields of Garvaghey
to see hawthorn on the summer
hedges, as though
he had never left;
a bend of the road

which still sheltered
primroses. But we
did not smile in
the shared complicity
of a dream, for when
weary Odysseus returns
Telemachus should leave.

Often as I descend
into subway or underground
I see his bald head behind
the bars of the small booth;
the mark of an old car
accident beating on his
ghostly forehead.

The Siege of Mullingar

At the Fleadh Cheoil in Mullingar
There were two sounds, the breaking
Of glass, and the background pulse
Of music. Young girls roamed
The streets with eager faces,
Shoving for men. Bottles in
Hand, they rowed out a song:
Puritan Ireland's dead and gone,
A myth of O'Connor and O'Faoláin.

In the early morning the lovers
Lay on both sides of the canal
Listening on Sony transistors
To the agony of Pope John.
Yet it didn't seem strange, or blasphemous,
This ground bass of death and
Resurrection, as we strolled along:
Puritan Ireland's dead and gone,
A myth of O'Connor and O'Faoláin.

Further on, breasting the wind
Waves of the deserted grain harbour
We saw a pair, a cob and his pen,
Most nobly linked. Everything then
In our casual morning vision
Seemed to flow in one direction,
Lines simple as a song:
Puritan Ireland's dead and gone,
A myth of O'Connor and O'Faoláin.

The Lure

for Sean O'Riada

Again, that note! A weaving
melancholy, like a bird crossing
moorland;
     pale ice on a corrie
opening inward, soundless harp-
strings of rain:
     the pathos
of last letters in the 1916 Room,
'Mother, I thank . . .'
      a podgy landmine.
Pearse's swordstick leading to a care-
fully profiled picture.
      That point
where folk and art meet, murmurs
Herr Doktor as
     the wail of tin
whistle climbs against fiddle, and
the *bodhrán* begins —
      lost cry
of the yellow bittern!

Tides

The window blown
open, that summer
night, a full moon

occupying the sky
with a pressure of
underwater light

a pale radiance
glossing the titles
behind your head

& the rectangle
of the bed where,
after long separation,

we begin to make
love quietly, bodies
turning like fish

in obedience to
the pull & tug
of your great tides.

King & Queen

Jagged head
of warrior, bird
of prey, surveying space

side by side
they squat, the pale
deities of this place

giant arms
slant to the calm
of lap, kneebone;

blunt fingers
splay to caress
a rain-hollowed stone

towards which
the landscape of five parishes
tends, band after band

of terminal,
peewit haunted,
cropless bogland.

The Wild Dog Rose

1

I go to say goodbye to the *cailleach,*
that terrible figure who haunted my childhood
but no longer harsh, a human being
merely, hurt by event.
                                The cottage,
circled by trees, weathered to admonitory
shapes of desolation by the mountain winds,
straggles into view. The rank thistles
and leathery bracken of untilled fields
stretch behind with — a final outcrop —
the hooped figure by the roadside,
its retinue of dogs
                            which give tongue
as I approach, with savage, whingeing cries
so that she slowly turns, a moving nest
of shawls and rags, to view, to stare
the stranger down.
                            And I feel again
that ancient awe, the terror of a child
before the great hooked nose, the cheeks
dewlapped with dirt, the staring blue
of the sunken eyes, the mottled claws
clutching a stick
                            but now hold
and return her gaze, to greet her,
as she greets me, in friendliness.
Memories have wrought reconciliation
between us, we talk in ease at last,
like old friends, lovers almost,
sharing secrets.
                            Of neighbours
she quarrelled with, who now lie
in Garvaghey graveyard, beyond all hatred;
of my family and hers, how she never married,

though a man came asking in her youth.
'You would be loath to leave your own,'
she sighs, 'and go among strangers' —
his parish ten miles off.

                      For sixty years
since she has lived alone, in one place.
Obscurely honoured by such confidences,
I idle by the summer roadside, listening,
while the monologue falters, continues,
rehearsing the small events of her life.
The only true madness is loneliness,
the monotonous voice in the skull
that never stops
                    because never heard.

2

And there
where the dogrose shines in the hedge
she tells me a story so terrible
that I try to push it away,
my bones melting.
                    Late at night
a drunk came, beating at her door
to break it in, the bolt snapping
from the soft wood, the thin mongrels
rushing to cut, but yelping as
he whirls with his farm boots
to crush their skulls.
                    In the darkness
they wrestle, two creatures crazed
with loneliness, the smell of the
decaying cottage in his nostrils
like a drug, his body heavy on hers,
the tasteless trunk of a seventy year
old virgin, which he rummages while

she battles for life
                              bony fingers
reaching desperately to push
against his bull neck. 'I prayed
to the Blessed Virgin herself
for help and after a time
I broke his grip.'
                              He rolls
to the floor, snores asleep,
while she cowers until dawn
and the dogs' whimpering starts
him awake, to lurch back across
the wet bog.

3
And still
the dogrose shines in the hedge.
Petals beaten wide by rain, it
sways slightly, at the tip of a
slender, tangled, arching branch
which, with her stick, she gathers
into us.
                    'The wild rose
is the only rose without thorns,'
she says, holding a wet blossom
for a second, in a hand knotted
as the knob of her stick.
'Whenever I see it, I remember
the Holy Mother of God and
all she suffered.'
                              Briefly
the air is strong with the smell
of that weak flower, offering
its crumbling yellow cup

and pale bleeding lips
fading to white
                    at the rim
of each bruised and heart-
shaped petal.

Special Delivery

The spider's web
of your handwriting
on a blue envelope

brings up too much
to bear, old sea-sick-
ness of love, retch

of sentiment, night
& day devoured by
the worm of delight

which turns to
feed upon itself;
emotion running so

wildly to seed
between us that
it assumes a third,

a ghost or child's
face, the soft skull
pale as an eggshell

& the life-cord
of the emerging body —
fish, reptile, bird —

which trails
like the cable
of an astronaut

as we whirl & turn
in our bubble of
blood & sperm

before the gravities
of earth claim us
from limitless space.

Now, light years later
your nostalgic letter
admitting failure,

claiming forgiveness.
When fire pales to
so faint an ash

so frail a design
why measure guilt
your fault or mine:

but blood seeps where
I sign before tearing
down the perforated line.

The Same Gesture

There is a secret room
of golden light where
everything — love, violence,
hatred is possible;
and, again, love.

Such intimacy of hand
and mind is achieved
under its healing light
that the shifting of
hands is a rite

like court music.
We barely know our
selves there though
it is what we always were
— most nakedly are —

and must remember
when we leave, re-
suming our habits
with our clothes:
work, 'phone, drive

through late traffic
changing gears with
the same gesture as
eased your snowbound
heart and flesh.

Last Journey

i.m. James Montague

We stand together
on the windy platform;
how crisp the rails
running out of sight
through the wet fields!

Carney, the station master,
is peering over
his frosted window:
the hand of the signal
points down.

Crowned with churns
a cart creaks up the
incline of Main Street
to the sliding doors
of the Co-Op.

A smell of coal,
the train is coming . . .
you climb slowly in,
propped by my hand to
a seat, away from the engine,

and we leave, waving
a plume of black smoke
over the rushy meadows,
small hills & hidden villages —
Beragh, Carrickmore,

Pomeroy, Fintona —
placenames that sigh
like a pressed melodeon
across this forgotten
Northern landscape.

Home Again

Lost in our separate work
We meet at dusk in a narrow lane.
I press back against a tree
To let him pass, but he brakes
Against our double loneliness
With: 'So you're home again!'

Catching a bus at Victoria Station,
Symbol of Belfast in its iron bleakness,
We ride through narrow huckster streets
(Small lamps bright before the Sacred Heart
Bunting tagged for some religious feast)
To where Cavehill and Divis, stern presences,
Brood over a wilderness of cinemas and shops,
Victorian red-brick villas, framed with aerials,
Bushmill hoardings, Orange and Legion Halls.
A fringe of trees affords some ease at last
From all this dour, despoiled inheritance,
The shabby through-otherness of outskirts:
'God is Love,' chalked on a grimy wall
Mocks a culture where constraint is all.

Through half of Ulster that Royal Road ran,
Through Lisburn, Lurgan, Portadown,
Solid British towns, lacking local grace.
Headscarved housewives in bulky floral skirts
Hugged market baskets on the rexine seats
Although it was near the borders of Tyrone —
End of a Pale, beginning of O'Neill —
Before a stranger turned a friendly face,
Yarning politics in Ulster monotone.
Bathos as we bumped all that twilight road,
Tales of the Ancient Order, Ulster's Volunteers:
Narrow fields wrought such division,

And narrow they were, though as darkness fell
Ruled by the evening star, which saw me home

To a gaunt farmhouse on this busy road,
Bisecting slopes of plaintive moorland,
Where I assume old ways of walk and work
So easily, yet feel the sadness of return
To what seems still, though changing.
No Wordsworthian dream enchants me here
With glint of glacial corrie, totemic mountain.
But merging low hills and gravel streams,
Oozy blackness of bog-banks, pale upland grass;
Rough Field in the Gaelic and rightly named
As setting for a mode of life that passes on:
Harsh landscape that haunts me,
Well and stone, in the bleak moors of dream.
With all my circling a failure to return.

1961

The Leaping Fire

i.m. Brigid Montague (1876-1966)

Each morning, from the corner
of the hearth, I saw a miracle
as you sifted the smoored ashes
to blow
     a fire's sleeping remains
back to life, holding the burning brands
of turf, between work hardened hands.
I draw on that fire . . . .

    3 OMAGH HOSPITAL
Your white hair
on the thin rack
of your shoulders

it is hard to
look into the eyes
of the dying

who carry away
a part of oneself —
a shared world

& you, whose life
was selflessness,
now die slowly

broken down by
process to a pale
exhausted beauty

the moon in her
last phase, caring
only for herself.

44

I lean over the
bed but you barely
recognize me &

when an image
forces entry —
Is that John?

Bring me home
you whimper &
I see a house

shaken by traffic
until a fault runs
from roof to base

but your face has
already retired into
the blind, animal

misery of age
paying out your
rosary beads

hands twitching
as you drift
towards nothingness

4 A HOLLOW NOTE

Family legend held
that this frail
woman had heard
the banshee's wail

& on the night
she lay dying
I heard a low,
constant crying

over the indifferent
roofs of Paris —
the marsh bittern
or white owl sailing

from its foul
nest of bones
to warn me with
a hollow note

& among autobuses
& taxis, the shrill
paraphernalia of a
swollen city

I crossed myself
from rusty habit
before I realised
why I had done it.

A Lost Tradition

All around, shards of a lost tradition:
From the Rough Field I went to school
In the Glen of the Hazels. Close by
Was the bishopric of the Golden Stone;
The cairn of Carleton's homesick poem.

Scattered over the hills, tribal-
And placenames, uncultivated pearls.
No rock or ruin, dun or dolmen
But showed memory defying cruelty
Through an image-encrusted name.

The heathery gap where the Rapparee,
Shane Barnagh, saw his brother die —
On a summer's day the dying sun
Stained its colours to crimson:
So breaks the heart, Brish-mo-Cree.

The whole landscape a manuscript
We had lost the skill to read,
A part of our past disinherited;
But fumbled, like a blind man,
Along the fingertips of instinct.

The last Gaelic speaker in the parish
When I stammered my school Irish
One Sunday after mass, crinkled
A rusty litany of praise:
Tá an Ghaeilge againn arís . . . .

Tír Eoghain: Land of Owen,
Province of the O'Niall;
The ghostly tread of O'Hagan's
Barefoot gallowglasses marching
To merge forces in Dun Geanainn

Push southward to Kinsale!
Loudly the war-cry is swallowed
In swirls of black rain and fog
As Ulster's pride, Elizabeth's foemen,
Founder in a Munster bog.

A Grafted Tongue

(Dumb,
bloodied, the severed
head now chokes to
speak another tongue —

As in
a long suppressed dream,
some stuttering garb-
led ordeal of my own)

An Irish
child weeps at school
repeating its English.
After each mistake

The master
gouges another mark
on the tally stick
hung about its neck

Like a bell
on a cow, a hobble
on a straying goat.
To slur and stumble

In shame
the altered syllables
of your own name:
to stray sadly home

And find
the turf-cured width
of your parents' hearth
growing slowly alien:

In cabin
and field, they still
speak the old tongue.
You may greet no one.

To grow
a second tongue, as
harsh a humiliation
as twice to be born.

Decades later
that child's grandchild's
speech stumbles over lost
syllables of an old order.

Seskilgreen

A circle of stones
surviving behind a
guttery farmhouse,

the capstone phallic
in a thistly meadow:
Seskilgreen Passage Grave.

Cup, circle,
triangle beating
their secret dance

(eyes, breasts,
thighs of a still
fragrant goddess).

I came last in May
to find the mound
drowned in bluebells

with a fearless wren
hoarding speckled eggs
in a stony crevice

while cattle
swayed sleepily
under low branches

lashing the ropes
of their tails
across the centuries.

Courtyard in Winter

Snow curls in on the cold wind.

Slowly, I push back the door.
After long absence, old habits
Are painfully revived, those disciplines
Which enable us to survive.
To keep a minimal fury alive
While flake by faltering flake

Snow curls in on the cold wind.

Along the courtyard, the boss
Of each cobblestone is rimmed
In white, with winter's weight
Pressing, like a silver shield,
On all the small plots of earth.
Inert in their living death as

Snow curls in on the cold wind.

Seized in a giant fist of frost,
The grounded planes at London Airport,
Mallarmé swans, trapped in ice.
The friend whom I have just left
Will be dead, a year from now
Through her own fault, while

Snow curls in on the cold wind.

Or smothered by some glacial truth?
Thirty years ago, I learnt to reach
Across the rusting hoops of steel
That bound our greening waterbarrel
To save the living water beneath
The hardening crust of ice, before

Snow curls in on the cold wind.

But despair has a deeper crust.
In all our hours together, I never
Managed to ease the single hurt
That edged her towards her death;
Never reached through her loneliness
To save a trust, chilled after

Snow curls in on the cold wind.

I plunged through snowdrifts once,
Above our home, to carry
A telegram to a mountain farm.
Fearful but inviting, they waved me
To warm myself at the flaring
Hearth before I faced again where

Snow curls in on the cold wind.

The news I brought was sadness.
In a far city, someone of their name
Lay dying. The tracks of foxes,
Wild birds as I climbed down
Seemed to form a secret writing
Minute and frail as life when

Snow curls in on the cold wind.

Sometimes, I know that message.
There is a disease called snow-sickness;
The glare from the bright god,
The earth's reply. As if that
Ceaseless, glittering light was
All the truth we'd left after

Snow curls in on the cold wind.

So, before dawn, comfort fails,
I imagine her end, in some sad
Bedsitting-room, the steady hiss
Of the gas more welcome than an
Act of friendship, the protective
Oblivion of a lover's caress if

Snow curls in on the cold wind.

In the canyon of the street
The dark snowclouds hesitate,
Turning to slush almost before
They cross the taut canvas of
The street stalls, the bustle
Of a sweeper's brush after

Snow curls in on the cold wind.

The walls are spectral, white.
All the trees black-ribbed, bare.
Only veins of ivy, the sturdy
Laurel with its waxen leaves,
Its scant red berries, survive
To form a winter wreath as

Snow curls in on the cold wind.

What solace but endurance, kindness?
Against her choice, I still affirm
That nothing dies, that even from
Such bitter failure memory grows;
The snowflake's structure, fragile
But intricate as the rose when

Snow curls in on the cold wind.

Dowager

I dwell in this leaky Western castle.
American matrons weave across the carpet,
Sorefooted as camels, and less useful.

Smooth Ionic columns hold up a roof.
A chandelier shines on a foxhound's coat:
The grandson of a grandmother I reared.

In the old days I read or embroidered,
But now it is enough to see the sky change,
Clouds extend or smother a mountain's shape.

Wet afternoons I ride in the Rolls;
Windshield wipers flail helpless against the rain:
I thrash through pools like smashing panes of glass.

And the light afterwards! Hedges steam,
I ride through a damp tunnel of sweetness,
The bonnet strewn with bridal hawthorn

From which a silver lady leaps, always young.
Alone, I hum with satisfaction in the sun,
An old bitch, with a warm mouthful of game.

The Errigal Road

We match paces along the Hill Head Road,
the road to the old churchyard of Errigal Keerogue;
its early cross, a heavy stone hidden in grass.

As we climb, my old Protestant neighbour
signals landmarks along his well trodden path,
some hill or valley celebrated in local myth.

'Yonder's Whiskey Hollow,' he declares,
indicating a line of lunar birches.
We halt to imagine men plotting

against the wind, feeding the fire or
smothering the fumes of an old fashioned worm
while the secret liquid bubbles & clears.

'And that's Foxhole Brae under there — '
pointing to the torn face of a quarry.
'It used to be crawling with them.'

(A red quarry slinks through the heather,
a movement swift as a bird's, melting as rain,
glimpsed behind a mound, disappears again.)

At Fairy Thorn Height the view fans out,
ruck and rise to where, swathed in mist
& rain, swells the mysterious saddle shape

of Knockmany Hill, its brooding tumulus
opening perspectives beyond our Christian myth.
'On a clear day you can see far into Monaghan,'

old Eagleson says, and we exchange sad notes
about the violence plaguing these parts;
last week, a gun battle outside Aughnacloy,

machine-gun fire splintering the wet thorns,
two men beaten up near dark Altamuskin,
an attempt to blow up Omagh Courthouse.

Helicopters overhead, hovering locusts.
Heavily booted soldiers probing vehicles, streets,
their strange antennae bristling, like insects.

At his lane's end, he turns to face me.
'Tell them down South that old neighbours
can still speak to each other around here'

& gives me his hand, but does not ask me in.
Rain misting my coat, I turn back towards
the main road, where cars whip smartly past

between small farms, fading back into forest.
Soon all our shared landscape will be effaced,
a quick stubble of pine recovering most.

Tearing

1
I sing your pain
as best I can
    seek
like a gentle man
    to assume
the proffered blame.

But the pose breaks.
The sour facts remain.
    It takes two
to make, one to break
    a marriage.
Unhood the falcon!

2 PASTOURELLE
Hands on the pommel,
long dress trailing
over polished leather
riding boots, a spur
jutting from the heel,
& beneath, the bridle path,
strewn with rusty apples,
brown knobs of chestnut,
meadow saffron and acorn.

Then we were in the high
ribbed dark of the trees
where animals move stealth-
ily, coupling & killing,

while we talked nostalgically
of our lives, bedevilled
& betrayed by lost love —
the furious mole, tunnelling
near us his tiny kingdom —

& how slowly we had come
to where we wished each other
happiness, far and apart, as
a hawk circled the wood,
& a victim cried, the sound
of hooves rising & falling
upon bramble & fern, while
a thin growth of rain gather-
ed about us, like a cowl.

3   NEVER
In the gathering dark
I caress your head
as you thrash out
flat words of pain:
'There is no way back,
I can feel it happening;
we shall never be
what we were, again'.

Never, a solemn bell
tolling through
that darkening room
where I cradle your head,

only a glimmer left
in the high window
over what was once
our marriage bed.

4   REFRAIN
I sit in autumn sunlight
on a hotel terrace as I did

when our marriage had begun,
our public honeymoon,

try to unsnarl what went wrong,
shouldering all the blame,

but no chivalric mode,
courtesy's silent discipline

softens the pain
when something is ending

and the tearing begins:
'We shall never be

what we were again'.
Old love's refrain.

No Music

I'll tell you a sore truth, little understood.
It's harder to leave, than to be left:
To stay, to leave, both sting wrong.

You will always have me to blame,
Can dream we might have sailed on;
From absence's rib, a warm fiction.

But I must recognise what I have done,
And if it fails, accept the burden
Of the harm done to you & another one.

To tear up old love by the roots,
To trample on past affections:
There is no music for so harsh a song.

Herbert Street Revisited

for Madeleine

1
A light is burning late
in this Georgian Dublin street:
someone is leading our old lives!

And our black cat scampers again
through the wet grass of the convent garden
upon his masculine errands.

The pubs shut: a released bull,
Behan shoulders up the street,
topples into our basement, roaring 'John!'

A pony and donkey cropped flank
by flank under the trees opposite;
short neck up, long neck down,

as Nurse Mullen knelt by her bedside
to pray for her lost Mayo hills,
the bruised bodies of Easter Volunteers.

Animals, neighbours, treading the pattern
of one time and place into history,
like our early marriage, while

tall windows looked down upon us
from walls flushed light pink or salmon
watching and enduring succession.

2

As I leave, you whisper,
'Don't betray our truth,'
and like a ghost dancer,
invoking a lost tribal strength,
I halt in tree-fed darkness

to summon back our past,
and celebrate a love that eased
so kindly, the dying bone,
enabling the spirit to sing
of old happiness, when alone.

3

So put the leaves back on the tree,
put the tree back in the ground,
let Brendan trundle his corpse down
the street singing, like Molly Malone.

Let the black cat, tiny emissary
of our happiness, streak again
through the darkness, to fall soft
clawed into a landlord's dustbin.

Let Nurse Mullen take the last
train to Westport, and die upright
in her chair, facing a window
warm with the blue slopes of Nephin.

And let the pony and donkey come —
look, someone has left the gate open —
like hobbyhorses linked in
the slow motion of a dream

parading side by side, down
the length of Herbert Street,
rising and falling, lifting
their hooves through the moonlight.

Blessing

A feel of warmth in this place.
In winter air, a scent of harvest.
No form of prayer is needed,
When by sudden grace attended.
Naturally, we fall from grace.
Mere humans, we forget what light
Led us, lonely, to this place.

Edge

Edenlike as your name
this sea's edge garden
where we rest, beneath
the clarity of a lighthouse.

To fly into risk,
attempt the dream,
cast off, as we have done,
requires true luck

who know ourselves
blessed to have found
between this harbour's arms
a sheltering home

where the vast
tides of the Atlantic
lift to caress
rose coloured rocks.

So fate relents.
Hushed and calm,
safe and secret,
on the edge is best.

The Well Dreams

1
The well dreams;
liquid bubbles.

Or it stirs
as a water spider skitters across;
a skinny legged dancer.

Sometimes, a gross interruption;
a stone plumps in.
That takes a while to absorb,
to digest, much groaning
and commotion in the well's stomach
before it can proffer again
an almost sleek surface.

Even a pebble disturbs
that tremor laden miniscus,
that implicit shivering.
They sink towards the floor,
the basement of quiet,
settle into a small mosaic.

And the single eye
of the well dreams on,
a silent cyclops.

2
People are different.
They live outside, insist
in their world of agitation.
A man comes by himself,
singing or in silence,
and hauls up his bucket slowly —

an act of meditation —
or jerks it up angrily,
like lifting a skin,
sweeping a circle
right through his own reflection.

3
And the well recomposes itself.

Crowds arrive annually, on pilgrimage.
Votive offerings adorn the bushes;
a child's rattle, hanging silent
(except when the wind shifts it)
a rag fluttering like a pennant.

Or a tarnished coin is thrown in,
sinking soundlessly to the bottom.
Water's slow alchemy washes it clean:
a queen of the realm, made virgin again.

4
Birds chatter above it.
They are the well's principal distraction,
swaying at the end of branches,
singing and swaying, darting excitement
of courting and nesting,
fending for the next brood,
who still seem the same robin,
thrush, blackbird or wren.

The trees stay silent.
The storms speak through them.
Then the leaves come sailing down,

sharp green or yellow,
betraying the seasons,
till a flashing shield of ice
forms over the well's single eye:
the year's final gift,
a static transparence.

5
But a well has its secret.
Under drifting leaves,
dormant stones around
the whitewashed wall,
the unpredictable ballet
of waterbugs, insects,

There the wellhead pulses,
little more than a tremor,
a flickering quiver,
spasms of silence;
small intensities of mirth,
the hidden laughter of earth.

The Silver Flask

Sweet, though short, our
hours as a family together.
Driving across dark mountains
to Midnight Mass in Fivemiletown,
lights coming up in the valleys
as in the days of Carleton.

Tussocks of heather brown
in the headlights; our mother
stowed in the back, a tartan
rug wrapped round her knees,
patiently listening as father sang,
and the silver flask went round.

Chorus after chorus of the *Adoremus*
to shorten the road before us,
till *we see amidst the winter's snows*
the festive lights of the small town
and from the choirloft an organ booms
Angels we have heard on high, with

my father joining warmly in,
his broken tenor soaring, faltering,
a legend in dim bars of Brooklyn
(that sacramental moment of stillness
among exiled, disgruntled men)
now raised vehemently once again

in the valleys he had sprung from,
startling the stiff congregation
with fierce blasts of song, while
our mother sat silent beside him,
sad but proud, an unaccustomed
blush mantling her wan countenance.

Then driving slowly home,
tongues crossed with the communion
wafer, snowflakes melting in
the car's hungry headlights,
till we reach the warm kitchen
and the spirits round again.

The family circle briefly restored
nearly twenty lonely years after
that last Christmas in Brooklyn,
under the same tinsel of decorations
so carefully hoarded by our mother
in the cabin trunk of a Cunard liner.

The Locket

Sing a last song
for the lady who has gone,
fertile source of guilt and pain.
The worst birth in the annals of Brooklyn,
that was my cue to come on,
my first claim to fame.

Naturally, she longed for a girl,
and all my infant curls of brown
couldn't excuse my double blunder
coming out, both the wrong sex,
and the wrong way around.
Not readily forgiven.

So you never nursed me
and when all my father's songs
couldn't sweeten the lack of money,
When poverty comes through the door
love flies up the chimney,
your favourite saying.

Then you gave me away,
might never have known me,
if I had not cycled down
to court you like a young man,
teasingly untying your apron,
drinking by the fire, yarning

Of your wild, young days
which didn't last long, for you,
lovely Molly, the belle of your small town,
landed up mournful and chill
as the constant rain that lashes it,
wound into your cocoon of pain.

Standing in that same hallway,
Don't come again, you say, roughly,
I start to get fond of you, John,
and then you are up and gone;
the harsh logic of a forlorn woman
resigned to being alone.

And still, mysterious blessing,
I never knew, until you were gone,
that, always around your neck,
you wore an oval locket
with an old picture in it,
of a child in Brooklyn.

Luggala

for Garech Browne

Again and again in dream, I return to that shore. There is a wind rising, a gull is trying to skim over the pines, and the waves whisper and strike along the bright sickle of the little strand. Shoving through reeds and rushes, leaping over a bogbrown stream, I approach the temple by the water's edge, death's shrine, cornerstone of your sadness. I stand inside, by one of the pillars of the mausoleum, and watch the water in the stone basin. As the wind ruffles cease, a calm surface appears, like a mirror or crystal. And into it your face rises, sad beyond speech, sad with an acceptance of blind, implacable process. For by this grey temple are three tombs, a baby brother, a half-sister and a grown brother, killed at twenty-one. Their monuments of Wicklow granite are as natural here as the scattered rocks, but there is no promise of resurrection, only the ultimate silence of the place, the shale littered face of the scree, the dark, dark waters of the glacial lake.

Discords

1

There is a white light in the room.
It is anger. He is angry, or
She is angry, or both are angry.
To them it is absolute, total,
It is everything; but to the visitor,
The onlooker, the outsider,
It is the usual, the absurd;
For if they did not love each other
Why should they heed a single word?

2

Another sad goodbye at the airport;
Neither has much to say, *en garde*,
Lest a chance word turn barbed.
You bring me, collect me, each journey
Not winged as love, but heavy as duty;
Lohengrin's swan dipping to Charon's ferry.

3

A last embrace at the door,
Your lovely face made ugly
By a sudden flush of tears
Which tell me more than any phrase,
Tell me what I most need to hear,
Wash away and cleanse my fears:
You have never ceased to love me.

The Hill of Silence

1
From the platform
of large raised stones

lines appear to lead us
along the hillside

bog tufts softening
beneath each step

bracken and briar
restraining our march

clawing us back, slowing
us to perception's pace.

2
A small animal halts,
starts, leaps away

and a lark begins
its dizzy, singing climb

towards the upper skies
and now another stone appears

ancient, looming, mossed
long ago placed,

lifted to be a signpost
along the old path.

3
Let us climb further.
As one thought leads
to another, so one lich-

ened snout of stone
still leads one on,
beckons to a final one.

4
Under its raised slab
thin trickles of water

gather to a shallow pool
in which the head stone

mirrors, and rears
to regard its shadow self,

and a diligent spider weaves
a trembling, silver web

a skein of terrible delicacy
swaying to the wind's touch

a fragile, silken scarf
a veined translucent leaf.

5
This is the slope of loneliness.
This is the hill of silence.
This is the winds' fortress.
Our world's polestar.
A stony patience.

6
We have reached a shelf
that surveys the valley

on these plains below
a battle flowed and ebbed

and the gored, spent warrior
was ferried up here

where water and herbs
might staunch his wounds.

7
Let us also lay ourselves
down in this silence

let us also be healed
wounds closed, senses cleansed

as over our bowed heads
the mad larks multiply

needles stabbing the sky
in an ecstasy of stitching fury

against the blue void
while from clump and tuft

cranny and cleft, soft footed
curious, the animals gather around.